FROM THE
LIBRARY

Reid

STEP BY STEP

A linked series of Board Books, Concept Books and Story Books
for the pre-school child

Board Books	*Concept Books*	*Story Books*
My House	Colours	Wet Paint
Day Time	Counting	Down in the Shed
Night Time	Noises	Over the Wall
Shopping	Big and Little	There and Back Again

First published 1988
by William Collins Sons & Co Ltd
in association with The Albion Press Ltd

© text Diane Wilmer 1988
© illustrations Nicola Smee 1988

British Library Cataloguing in Publication Data
Wilmer, Diane
  Counting. — (Step-by-step).
  1. Readers — 1950–
  I. Title II. Smee, Nicola III. Series
  428.6   PE1119

ISBN 0-00-181126-6

All rights reserved. No part of this publication may be reproduced, stored in a retrieval system, or transmitted, in any form or by any means, electronic, mechanical, photocopying, recording or otherwise, without the prior permission of William Collins Sons & Co Ltd, 8 Grafton Street, London W1X 3LA.

Printed and bound in Hong Kong by South China Printing Co

STEP BY STEP

Counting

Diane Wilmer
illustrated by Nicola Smee

COLLINS
in association with THE ALBION PRESS

Time for bed.
What a mess!

Into the toybox goes

 big drum

2 shiny robots

3 sailing boats

4 tired dollies

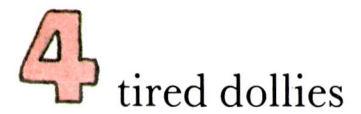

5 wild animals

6 wax crayons

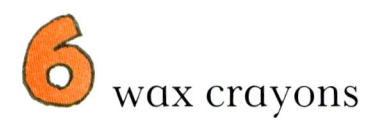

7 trucks

7

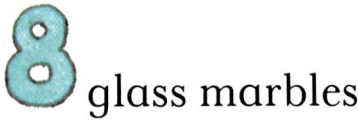 glass marbles

9 building blocks

and **10** smart soldiers

marching off to bed.

Goodnight.